The Keeper of the Gate

*Unlocking the Secrets of Being
Prepared for Your Next Family Crisis*

BETH HENRY

First published by Ultimate World Publishing 2024
Copyright © 2024 Beth Henry

ISBN

Paperback: 978-1-923123-62-5
Ebook: 978-1-923123-63-2

Beth Henry has asserted her rights under the Copyright, Designs and Patents Act 1988 to be identified as the author of this work. The information in this book is based on the author's experiences and opinions. The publisher specifically disclaims responsibility for any adverse consequences which may result from use of the information contained herein. Permission to use information has been sought by the author. Any breaches will be rectified in further editions of the book.

All rights reserved. No part of this publication may be reproduced, stored in or introduced into a retrieval system, or transmitted in any form, or by any means (electronic, mechanical, photocopying, recording or otherwise) without the prior written permission of the author. Any person who does any unauthorized act in relation to this publication may be liable to criminal prosecution and civil claims for damages. Enquiries should be made through the publisher.

Cover design: Ultimate World Publishing
Layout and typesetting: Ultimate World Publishing
Editor: Carmela Julian Valencia

Ultimate World Publishing
Diamond Creek,
Victoria Australia 3089
www.writeabook.com.au

Contents

Introduction. 1

Chapter 1: Your Basic Information Key 9

Chapter 2: Family Information Key 13

Chapter 3: Your Health Information Key 17

Chapter 4: Your Family's Health Information Key 23

Chapter 5: Employment & Financial Details Key 31

Chapter 6: Property Information Key 37

Chapter 7: Professional Information Key 45

Afterword 51

Introduction

When I wrote *The Family Connection Guide,* it was specifically geared to our generation to help us get ahead of a stressful family situation with our aging parents. Having experienced *unexpected* emergencies with my clients as a real estate agent and as a daughter in my own family, I understood that having essential information for those life events is vital.

Mom or Dad has had a fall or an allergic reaction to a new medication or more seriously, a stroke or heart attack.

If you haven't had a chance to read *The Family Connection Guide: Everything You Need to Know About Getting Ahead of a Stressful Family Situation*, follow this link to get your copy today – www.thefamilyconnectionguide.com

As I was waiting for my book to be published, I had an aha moment. I need to apply these basic rules for us—our generation—for our husbands or wives and kids.

Oh, the kids! They really don't know how we do what we do, right? They just come to us for stuff—a lot of stuff. I'm not saying they don't know anything, but they don't know what they don't know, only that Mom or Dad can help and get it done. And our significant others—my husband knows that my laptop is blue, and that's it! Well, I actually had to tell him that it's blue, but in his defence I only know that his equipment is green and yellow and that he spends a lot of time at John Deere. Yes, he's a farmer, and I won't pretend to know the behind the scenes of his days of planting and harvesting or the maintaining of the equipment, but I am his bookkeeper, and I keep it straight for him with help from our accountants.

THE KEEPER OF THE GATE

What I'm saying is that I'm the go-to person in my family, the Keeper of the Gate!

There's usually that one person in a relationship who takes care of it all—the planning, the buying of groceries, the banking, scheduling time to get the oil changed and getting together with friends. Maybe you are the go-to person, the Keeper of the Gate.

Do any of these statements sound familiar?

> Mom, do you know where my backpack is?
> Honey, do you know where I put my keys?
> What time do I have to be there? Can you drive me?
> I'm not ready yet!

INTRODUCTION

Mom, the dog threw up!
How much do I owe?
Got any cash?

If any of this resonates with you, you're the go-to person in your life and you're going to love this guide!

It's a little more detailed than the calendar we get from our local real estate agent at Christmas or the local pet store with those stickers we can stick on a particular date to remind us that the dog needs his pills or of our next dentist appointment.

Listen, we're all organized, or at least we try to be. We have to be to get through our very long days, because if we're not, we can walk into scenes like this!

When I underwent a day surgery, I made sure that all the banking, laundry and domestics (house cleaning) were done, as I knew I would be off my feet for a few days up to a week or more. But for one reason or another, I freaked myself out and started to wonder, *What if I was in the hospital longer than expected for whatever reason? Could my husband temporarily pick up where I left off?*

THE KEEPER OF THE GATE

My mind started racing. *I'd better let him in on a few things I've been taking care of or waiting on. No, I need to write it all down for him.*

Like I mentioned before, he knows my laptop is blue but doesn't know how to log on! He's not the techie kinda guy; he would call one of our close friends and ask them to help. But would they know how to log on? I'm sure they would try to figure it out, but there would be a lot of stress tied to it, and ultimately give up and wait till I was able to do it. But what would that look like for me in 30 or 60 days from now?

It reminded me of the days when I worked in an office environment and had a week's holiday coming. I would write down every detail of my day-to-day and how to get my assigned tasks done for the person filling in for me. One time, I remember not really doing a good job of detailing it because I rushed and really didn't care about it all; I was going on holidays! I procrastinated, I only knew when my holidays were, oh, I don't know since the beginning of the year, when I had to book my holidays with my boss!

When I returned from my well-deserved holiday, it took me almost two weeks to get back on track again with my job. It was a nightmare. Some of you, I'm sure, have experienced this kind of mess and know exactly what I'm talking about. Maybe you have heard the old saying, "It's going to take me two weeks to get organized, so I can take a week off."

Feeling the stress that was building as I thought about it all, I decided to take my own advice, took *The Family Connection Guide* forms and filled them out. I skipped the lines that didn't apply to my family life and added a few that did. It was so relieving to have that information in place for my husband and kids if I was unfortunately required to stay in the hospital for a longer period of time.

Good news: There were no issues after surgery, and I was sent home that afternoon.

After a few days of recovering, I created a few new forms that fit around my family life and our generational events, as we are the Keepers of the Gate. I wear

INTRODUCTION

many hats, as I'm sure you do. We always seem to be looking for that extra hour in the day.

I want you to ask yourself another question.

Do you have a plan? Is it written down somewhere if you were unable to do what you do?

Then, think about passwords.

When I thought about passwords, I realized that I have over 60 passwords, usernames and secret questions for everything—from banking and shopping websites to emails and device logins. How many do you think you have? Please don't tell me that you use the same password for everything you log on to! That's another book!

What about appointments and schedules? If you're like many of us, you have things scheduled for six months from now. Does anyone in your family know those details? Would those appointments be met or at least cancelled and rescheduled so you wouldn't be charged a no-show fee?

Our kids have grown up and have homes and children of their own now. However, I have many friends who have adult children still living at home with them and are very busy trying to keep it all together and in order, sort of. They do things that they are not even aware of anymore, because they've done them for so long. As the saying goes, "I can do it with my eyes closed."

If you have minor-aged children or a child with disabilities, you're going to need a plan for them. They may be a little or a lot off without you and your routine, but having a plan will ease the stress for them, having it all taken care of by the next best person.

This book is intended for temporary issues—a day or two, maybe a week or so when you are unable to be the Keeper of the Gate. For longer and more difficult issues and delays, there needs to be something prepared if you are no longer able to do what you do. Think about that for a moment. If you were unable to do what you do for everyone in your family, indefinitely, what would that look like? I don't want to be the doomsday person or scare you, but we all need to have a plan in place for those unexpected life events. I go into more detail in Chapter 7: Professional Information Key.

My husband and I may not have the kids at home anymore, but we still have very busy lives with our own businesses and life in general. I used to write in a Day-Timer planner to keep things in order, but now I have alarms set in my cell so I don't forget the things I need to remember; I'm sure you have noticed that there is so much more to remember these days. Some days I can't keep it all straight, so it's very convenient and a great tool for my toolbox.

Organized people like us are always keeping an eye out for tools to help with our very busy days. With that in mind, I have created *The Keeper of the Gate*, a short, easy-to-read guide with fillable forms. It's a fantastic addition to your toolbox for those *unexpected* emergencies. Once you complete them, you and everyone involved in your life will have that vital information in a moment's notice!

You can complete the forms and print them off, like an edition of your Life for Dummies, or you can e-mail it to your significant other or a close friend who can

INTRODUCTION

navigate a computer. This will be instrumental for them to follow, if need be, to keep things in your family life moving along smoothly while you are recovering and unable to cross out things on your very long to-do list.

Maybe you have already dealt with a situation like this. Do you remember the stress of not knowing how to manage it all? Did the bills get paid on time? Did you know where the important documents were? Did you know about the scheduled appointments?

What if you were the one who had to stay in the hospital longer than you expected? Could your significant other pick up where you left off? It's definitely something to think about, and this guide will show you how to get ahead of a stressful family situation, step by step. I made the time, and so should you!

If you're single, you definitely need to get organized. Being single can be just as busy as having a family to take care of. If you're married or have a significant other, you will most definitely need to be better prepared to keep things moving smoothly for you and your family. If you are a single parent, you have to have this in your toolbox.

Start now. Stress comes from ignoring things that you shouldn't be ignoring. Don't stick your head in the sand and tell yourself there's time. Break the task down into smaller tasks. In this case, chapter by chapter. Don't wait to be in the right mood. Motivation creates actions.

Just get started. You'll find your motivation.

Get better prepared for an *unexpected* emergency. If not for your own sanity, for your family's.

Chapter 1

Your Basic Information Key

This form is for you, for your basic details. As I have said before, your basic details streamline the emergency response. But before you sit down to complete the forms, carve out an hour just to read it through. It's only 50 or so pages-long, including the forms. It will get you in the right mindset of what you need to do and how much better you will feel making the time to get the forms completed.

My advice, do it in the daytime or with your morning coffee. I say this because when I was writing *The Family Connection Guide* and worked on it in the evening after dinner, I didn't get a good night's sleep. Let me rephrase that, I couldn't fall asleep. My mind wouldn't shut down and become quiet. It would come up with all kinds of ideas or things that I needed to do or things I forgot to do, and I would find myself trying to be quiet in the middle of the night, writing notes.

People have suggested keeping a pen and paper beside my bed, so I can jot down my thoughts. That's a great idea, but I don't want to wake up my husband, so that really doesn't work for me.

On those nights, my husband would say, "Just shut your mind off like a switch!"

He has no issues falling asleep. He knows where his switch is; I'm still looking for mine! Maybe it is true—men are from Mars, women are from Venus! LOL!

Whatever time works for you, just make the time, chapter by chapter. Give yourself an hour or so for each one, so you have the information you need to fill out the forms. I don't want you to get all excited filling the forms out, then stalling because you have to go look for the relevant documents and then have a squirrel moment. I'm sure you have had that kind of moment—asking yourself, "What did I walk in this room for?" and ending up doing something totally different from why you walked into the room in the first place. Am I right? LOL!

Entering the date will remind you when you filled these forms out.

You may need to get your wallet out to get your driver's licence number and the like, but that's probably it. My husband knows his driver's licence off by heart and finds it funny that I don't. I've tried to remember it, but my brain is full, and I don't need to memorize it. There's a whole lot to remember these days, and that's not one of them!

Many of us don't have a landline any longer, but some of us (like me) still do. I've kept it for those just-in-case moments, and of course, I still have a fax machine but can't remember the last time I actually faxed something. I might have to rethink that decision.

Have someone witness these forms. Make sure someone close to you knows these forms exist. If you do have an unfortunate emergency or have to be out of the game temporarily, the people in your life will be less stressed, knowing that you have a plan for them to take the reins while you recover. You will also be able to recover with less stress, knowing that things are running smoothly, probably not as well as you would do things, because you are the Keeper of the Gate!

If some of the lines do not apply to your life, just skip them.

YOUR BASIC INFORMATION KEY

Today's Date: _____

Given Name: _____

Birthdate: _____ Birth City/Province: _____

Birth Country: _____ Citizenship: _____

Social Insurance Number: _____

Health Card Number: _____

Drivers Licence Number: _____

E-mail: _____

Address: _____

City: _____ Province: _____ Postal Code: _____

Telephone #: _____ Cell #: _____

Military Service: _____

Religious Affiliation: _____

Contact Name: _____ Contact #: _____

Forms completed by: _____ Date: _____

Relationship: _____

Witnessed by: _____ Date: _____

Relationship: _____

Chapter 2

Family Information Key

This next form is for your family—your spouse, significant other and children. Again, give yourself an hour or so to read through this chapter and have a look at the forms. Get the information you need and have it all there on the table before you start. It'll be a lot more organized, and you will feel a lot more organized.

If you're separated or divorced, your ex may not want their details noted, but at least have their name and contact information, in case there is a matter they need to be involved with.

Is your spouse or significant other involved with the military? If so, have that contact information noted, especially if they are serving overseas—and please thank them for me. I don't think our military personnel hear that enough.

If you are involved with your church, have their contact information available. Your church members can be of a great help if the need arises.

I've also included a line for other contact details. This could be a trusted friend, a neighbour, your parents or your ICE (In Case of Emergency) contact. We should all have our ICE contact details in our cells. It is recognized by emergency medical technicians (EMTs), firefighters, emergency personnel and others who deal with accidents, fires and other types of emergencies all over the world.

Android and iPhone devices have instructions on how to add these important contact details to your device. If you haven't already added your ICE contact to your cell, look it up online and make the time *now* to add it to your device. Even if your cell is locked, the emergency personnel can still get in touch with your ICE. My cell has the option to add medical details if I want. Some of you already know this and have this in place, but many people don't.

I've also included a line for our other family members, our pets! Make sure you include their details and have a plan for them too. My boys were very much a part of my day-to-day. We know a lot of people in our town, but I think a lot more people know us because of them, Deeks and Gibbs.

YOUR FAMILY INFORMATION KEY

Single: ____ Widowed: ____ Divorced: ____ Common-Law: ____ Married: ____

Marriage Date: _____ City of Marriage: _____

Name of Spouse: _____

Spouse Birthdate: _____ Birth City: _____

Spouse Health Card #: _____

Spouse Social Insurance #: _____

Spouse E-mail: _____

Spouse Cell #: _____

Spouse Work Info: _____

Military Service: _____

Religious Affiliation: _____

Contact Name: _____ Contact #: _____

Children Names: _____
_____

(See Chapter 2 for children's details)

Other Contact Name: _____

Contact #: _____ E-mail: _____

Pets: Yes ___ No ___ Names: _____

Veterinary: _____ Contact #: _____

Details: _____
_____
_____

(examples: medications, dog walker, doggy daycare info)

Chapter 3

Your Health Information Key

This form is for you and your health details. This form is very simple to complete but so very important. This page gives you the ability to share all that information you have stored in your brain! These details you know by heart—when your last doctor appointment was, what pharmacy you use for yourself and the family.

If you're anything like me, you do remember most appointments you have been to over the years, but as you get older, you do forget a few things, like your last mammogram or what medication you had to take for an ailment.

Are you allergic to a particular drug? Does aspirin or ibuprofen upset your stomach? I am allergic to Demerol, as it makes me violently ill. I know that, but if I'm not able to communicate that to the emergency team, they will definitely be cleaning things up, if you know what I mean. I did hear from a nurse at my day surgery that most hospitals have stopped using Demerol and have replaced it with another drug.

These details will give everyone involved your essential medical history if you are unable to communicate with the emergency teams. Having the pharmacy you use will allow them to check any medications you may be taking or not taking. This can literally be life-saving information. I have learned in my research that many complications, including drug reactions, happen in emergency departments because they don't have the patient's medical history.

Some people don't know their blood type. There are many different ways to get that information—ask your parents, use at-home blood kits, donate blood, take saliva tests available at the drug store, contact your doctor and—I just learned—it may be noted on your birth certificate. Please ensure you know your blood type.

Being an organ donor is a wonderful decision. One organ donor can save up to eight lives! Here in Canada, you need to be registered as an organ donor. In Ontario, there is a registration form that comes with your driver's licence. Check where you live for further details, as the registration process is different for every province, state and country.

If you do have health insurance through your place of employment, please make note of their details. Each insurance company has different requirements for making a claim. If you have purchased your own independent health insurance, give them a call and make sure you understand their requirements and have an up-to-date policy.

The Medical Details page is a bit of history of past and present medications, allergies or surgeries you have experienced or are presently dealing with.

YOUR HEALTH INFORMATION KEY

Family Doctor Name: _____

Tel #: _____ E-mail: _____

Pharmacy Info: _____ Tel #: _____

Specialist Name: _____

Tel #: _____ E-mail: _____

Dentist Name: _____

Tel #: _____ E-mail: _____

Eye Glasses? Yes ___ No ___ Optometrist Name: _____

Tel #: _____ E-mail: _____

Blood Type: _____ Organ Donor? Yes __ No __ Completed Forms: Yes __ No __

Hearing Aid: Yes __ No __ Artificial Limbs: Yes __ No __

Independent Health Insurance: Yes ___ No ___

Company: _____ Tel #: _____

Policy #: _____ Plan & Client ID #: _____

List health concerns or challenges: *More space on next page*

_____

_____

_____

_____

_____

MEDICAL DETAILS

For: _____

| *Medications* | *Reason* | *Date started* |

_____
_____
_____
_____
_____
_____
_____
_____
_____

Surgeries: _____
_____
_____
_____

Allergies: _____
_____
_____

Recent challenges or concerns: _____
_____
_____

Chapter 4

Your Family's Health Information Key

I wasn't going to have a page for your spouse/partner or significant other's medical details, but I thought if you were unable to offer everything that you knew off by heart about them, this page would definitely help bridge the gap if the need did arise. If you have no significant other, just skip this section.

I'm not sure how the medical staffing is in your area, but here in Ontario—and, well, pretty much all of Canada—we seem to have a bit of a shortage of medical professionals these days, even before the pandemic. Our doctors, and especially our nurses, have left their profession for many different reasons. I don't want to get into a political discussion here, but we don't have as many as we once did, and there seem to be many more of us looking for a doctor these days. I remember when one family had one family doctor or one medical center to visit other than a specialist if one of us needed one.

I've been lucky to have the same doctor since my early twenties. On the other hand, my husband's doctor retired a few years back, and he hasn't been able to find a doctor in our area since. He has been on a few waiting lists but still no call to be added to that doctor's care. So, in the meantime, he has seen a nurse practitioner—who is great, by the way—for his medical exams to keep up to date with his AZ licence.

If your partner doesn't have a doctor or hasn't been seen by any medical team, please write that down, but do enter the last doctor they saw and when. It may not be needed, but the more information the better.

Do you know their blood type? Are they an organ donor with completed forms?

Most of my friends know their blood type but really haven't thought about being an organ donor and are not sure how to go about it. As I have mentioned earlier, there's a form that comes with your driver's licence here in Ontario. If you're not sure, ask your doctor or look it up online.

Your partner may have health insurance through their employer or have purchased their own through a private provider. Please make sure you have the correct information and complete this line on the form, as I have learned through my research that many challenges come up if there isn't a clear picture regarding health insurance.

Here in Ontario, we have OHIP (Ontario Health Insurance Plan), which covers any visits to a doctor or emergency room, if you are a resident of Ontario. We do pay for it on our yearly tax filing forms, but things are changing for this plan and some previously covered items are no longer covered. If you are in Ontario, check the OHIP website (www.ontario.ca) for a clearer picture on what is covered.

I have given you two separate pages for your children's details.

There is enough space for each child's school and teacher's information. If they are bussed to school, there's a place for those details too.

I have also created a line for any current health concerns. If your child is taking any type of medication that needs to be taken throughout the day while at school, make note of that on this line. I'm sure the school nurse or the teacher has already been made aware of this, but the person who is taking care of things for you may not, so please make sure you have this noted.

Their doctor/pediatrician's contact information has a place too.

I have also made room for their outside activities. If your kids are anything like mine were, you're going to need it.

It's been a while since I had to look at a calendar on the fridge to figure out what time and field I had to have the kids at for a practice or a game. I used to keep a calendar on the fridge before our cells became our assistants or our pains in the butt, whichever way you look at the new technology. I also had a calendar taped to my son's bedroom door as a reminder for him and me whenever I went into his room. But if you do have a calendar on the fridge, take a picture of it; if it's in a digital form, send it to your emergency contact, or at least make it shareable so that they can pick up where you left off. Also, if your child has certain likes and dislikes, make note of them. This will go a long way to keep the stress at a minimum for your child and the person taking care of things for you.

You can also use the Additional Details pages at the back of this book if you need more room.

YOUR PARTNER'S HEALTH INFORMATION KEY

Family Doctor Name: _____

Tel #: _____ E-mail: _____

Pharmacy Info: _____ Tel #: _____

Specialist Name: _____

Tel #: _____ E-mail: _____

Dentist Name: _____

Tel #: _____ E-mail: _____

Eye Glasses? Yes ___ No ___ Optometrist Name: _____

Tel #: _____ E-mail: _____

Blood Type: _____ Organ Donor? Yes__ No__ Completed Forms: Yes __ No __

Hearing Aid: Yes __ No __ Artificial Limbs: Yes __ No __

Independent Health Insurance: Yes ___ No ___

Company: _____ Tel #: _____

Policy #: _____ Plan & Client ID #: _____

List health concerns or challenges: *More space on next page*

_____

_____

_____

_____

_____

YOUR PARTNER'S MEDICAL DETAILS

For: _____

Medications　　　　　　　*Reason*　　　　　　　*Date started*

_____

_____

_____

_____

_____

_____

_____

_____

_____

_____

Surgeries: _____

_____

_____

_____

Allergies: _____

_____

_____

Recent challenges or concerns: _____

_____

_____

YOUR CHILDREN'S INFORMATION

Child's Name: _____ Birthdate: _____

School Name: _____ Tel #: _____

Grade: _____ Teacher's Name: _____

School Transportation Company _____

Bus #: ___ Location: _____ Pickup Time: _____ Drop off: _____

Health Concerns: _____

Doctor/Pediatrician: _____ Contact #: _____

Outside Activities: _____
(Hockey/Baseball/Soccer/Dance/Guides/Scouts/Tutoring)

_____

_____

Child's Name: _____ Birthdate: _____

School Name: _____ Tel #: _____

Grade: _____ Teacher's Name: _____

School Transportation Company _____

Bus #: ___ Location: _____ Pickup Time: _____ Drop off: _____

Health Concerns: _____

Doctor/Pediatrician: _____ Contact #: _____

Outside Activities: _____
(Hockey/Baseball/Soccer/Dance/Guides/Scouts/Tutoring)

_____

_____

(If you need more space for details, please use the back pages)

YOUR CHILDREN'S INFORMATION

Child's Name: _____ Birthdate: _____

School Name: _____ Tel #: _____

Grade: _____ Teacher's Name: _____

School Transportation Company _____

Bus #: ___ Location: _____ Pickup Time: _____ Drop off: _____

Health Concerns: _____

Doctor/Pediatrician: _____ Contact #: _____

Outside Activities: _____
(Hockey/Baseball/Soccer/Dance/Guides/Scouts/Tutoring)

_____
_____

Child's Name: _____ Birthdate: _____

School Name: _____ Tel #: _____

Grade: _____ Teacher's Name: _____

School Transportation Company _____

Bus #: ___ Location: _____ Pickup Time: _____ Drop off: _____

Health Concerns: _____
Doctor/Pediatrician: _____ Contact #: _____
Outside Activities: _____
(Hockey/Baseball/Soccer/Dance/Guides/Scouts/Tutoring)

_____
_____

(If you need more space for details, please use the back pages)

Chapter 5

Employment & Financial Details Key

I was going to break this chapter down into two, but after thinking it through, I realized it's pretty much self-explanatory.

Having your employer's contact information to notify them that you will not be in will cut down the legwork for whoever is looking after things for you. If you are self-employed like my husband and me, you understand there is a lot of "backstage" for the self-employed—you are every department of the business! The Keeper of the Gate of your business! You know the Who, What, When, Where, Why and How.

Think about that for a moment. Does anyone else know those details?

I manage the books for our lives and our businesses. There are a couple of spreadsheets that I update on a quarterly basis, time-sensitive government entries on a monthly basis and, well, I do everything but operate the farm equipment.

Being involved with the real estate world, there is a lot to keep up with everything that is changing, and there's a lot these days. If you are self-employed, you know exactly what I'm speaking of. There's a lot of behind-the-scenes kind of stuff.

If you were unavailable to complete these tasks, even for a short period of time, it would get backed up very quickly and become a nightmare for you later on. But, good news: I am in the middle of an outline for another book for the self-employed! I believe this is something that every self-employed person needs.

In the meantime, dedicate one of the last Additional Details pages to describe your daily tasks and how to go about them or write down the contact number of the person who does know how to go about things for your business and stay tuned for my pre-launch of that book.

OK, back to this chapter!

Reach out to your bank and have a discussion to find out what they need to help you keep things running smoothly while you are not available in an emergency. They are happy to help you, but in the meantime, enter your chequing and savings account numbers, LOC (line of credit) information and any other accounting information available. If you are feeling uneasy about having this information written down, call your bank and have that discussion with them. If you have it all in place, there's no need to write that information, but note down the name of the person who set it all up for you along with their telephone number and extension. It will make things so much easier and less stressful.

If your mortgage is with another institution other than your bank, give them a call and see what they can do if the need arises. Same with your credit cards.

Remember, this is about keeping the stress levels to a minimum while you are dealing with an emergency.

You may have other streams of income besides your full-time job. It could be a side gig or hustle or a part-time job. If you think it's worth noting and something that has to be taken care of while you are unable to, make a note of it on the "Other Types of Income" line.

You may have disability income that can vary from province, state or country. There are many government programs available—EI (employment insurance

EMPLOYMENT & FINANCIAL DETAILS KEY

for those who lost their jobs), WSIB (workers' compensation program), SSI (Supplemental Security Income) and LTD (Long-Term Disability). You may also have your own private insurance that sends you income from a previous accident or disability. There are many different types, and if any of them apply to your situation, please make note of them along with the type, Client ID numbers or Plan numbers and contact information.

If you're caregiving for someone as a part-time job or as a simple neighbourly gesture, a friend suggested having a plan for that person too. For instance, this could be a close friend you pick up on a specific day to run errands with because they don't drive, or an elderly neighbour whom you check on or shop for weekly because they can't do it themselves. Please make sure that you note these responsibilities you have taken on. Depending on the length of time that you are out of the game, other arrangements may have to be made until you are up and doing well again.

Again, if none of these apply to your situation, just skip them.

Having more information is always better. The idea behind these pages is to have the information at the ready in case the need comes up. However, if you experience changes in your circumstances (such as a disability), it is important that *you* communicate these changes to the insurance provider. Do not rely on others to do this for you. Please make sure that you pass on the information with a direct phone call or e-mail with the insurance or government program.

I had an associate, many years ago, who had an accident at home while on workers' compensation. His wife knew that they had insurance through work and let the administration at his office take care of the particulars. For some reason or another, the Workers' Compensation Board was not notified that there was an accident at home. It was a complete nightmare for the family.

EMPLOYMENT & FINANCIAL INFORMATION KEY

Employed: Yes___ No___ Self Employed____

Company Name: _____

Address: _____

Contact Tel #: _____ Manager: _____

Bank: _____

Address: _____

Tel #: _____ Bank Manager: _____

Chequing Account #: _____

Savings Account #: _____

Line of Credit #: _____

Mortgage: Yes___ No___ Mortgage Acct #: _____

Mortgage Company: _____

Mortgage Contact #: _____

Credit Card #: _____

Credit Card #: _____

Safety Deposit Box: Yes___ No___ Key Location: _____

RRSP: Yes___ No___ Plan #: _____

Other Types of Income: _____

Disability Info: _____

_____

Type: _____ Contact #: _____

Plan or Client ID #: _____

(If you need more space for details, please use the back pages)

Chapter 6

Property Information Key

This form is self-explanatory and can be very helpful if you need it in a pinch. If you don't have the details, actual account number or contact information for any issues you may have at any given time, it's great for reference.

Again, please take a moment and read through this chapter. Have a look at the form and get that information ready on the table so that when you are completing the forms, you will have everything at your fingertips, with no reason to go hunting for the documents and have another squirrel moment.

If you own your home, your home has a Property Roll number, which is usually a 10 to 18-digit number. This is basically the number that identifies your home to your town or city, and it is required when calling the town or city hall and paying your property taxes. It will be helpful for the person who is looking after things if they need to call. Having this number noted will help them get the information on your property taxes, when they are due and if they have been paid and up to date.

If you rent, having the landlord's contact number will give the person looking after things the ability to contact the landlord if something needs to be repaired if they are unable to.

Mailbox location and box number are important if you are the only one who collects the mail. As I mentioned in *The Family Connection Guide*, here in Ontario, Canada, our mail is redirected to super mailbox locations and not delivered to our physical addresses any longer, so you need to have this information entered. I have a picture of the actual super mailbox, box number and the street where it is located, just in case I need someone to pick up our mail while we are away. If you live in an apartment building, please note the location and box number.

My husband had to pick up the mail while I was away for a few days, and it took him a bit longer than he thought to figure out what box number the key would fit into. He hasn't picked up the mail in years. He knew the location of the super mailbox but wasn't sure what box number. He then realized that they had added a few more boxes to our location, and he couldn't tell which one was ours. He knew which row our mailbox was in, but with the additions, he wasn't sure of the actual mailbox. I didn't even think of telling him what number it was, I thought he knew. Oh, and to answer your question: Yes, he thought about calling me to ask, but he kept trying and eventually got our mail.

Having your property insurance broker's information is important as well. Many insurance companies these days consider a property vacant if no one is living there for more than 30 days. It's worth a call to get their rules and regulations under your policy.

Utility companies can get complicated when it comes to who and what they will communicate to the person calling for billing details or repairs. They may be able to help, depending on what your profile has in place. Again, it's worth a call to get their rules and regulations on having something in place if the need arises. I have had a few occasions where one utility company wouldn't give me any information because my name was not on the billing profile, while others sent a text to the number on the profile to verify they were speaking to the person who has authorization to make any changes. Some utility companies would also process a request or give information without any verification, so please make sure your profile with these companies is up to date.

You may have a cottage or trailer that you get to escape to on the weekends and holidays. Make sure you note any particulars, such as any utility companies or if there are fees that are due at the park where you camp. Note the due date, the contact number of a neighbour or the trailer park management—anything that will

PROPERTY INFORMATION KEY

help others take care of things for you while you can't. Some of the things we do are so second nature to us that we forget about them.

Speaking of escapes to the cottage or a vacation/holiday to another country or just simply away from home for any period of time, I need to bring up passports and travel itineraries. It is important to let someone you trust have this information.

Travel itineraries should include the airline, hotel or Airbnb, and whatever your plans are, including the time you're leaving and expected back home. In the event that something goes south, they will have the details to help or assist you if the need arises. It's just a good thing to do.

Some of you may not feel comfortable in having their passport information written down, and you're not wrong. There are many ways for thieves and scammers to steal your identity and do many things with it. But, having a copy of your passport can help you if it is lost. In some countries, it is necessary for the hotel to have your passport details and report them to the local authorities. It's just the way things are done. Having copies of your passport and credit cards is a helpful step if your wallet is lost or stolen.

I did not make a line for this information. I just wanted to bring this subject up, as it is another way to help you be less stressed, especially if you are going away for a well-deserved holiday.

If you have a vehicle or other types of motor vehicles, like sleds, motorcycles, dirt bikes, boats and the like, please note those details. It may not be an issue, but the more information, the better.

The next page is for those password-protected properties we have. Our laptops, tablets, cell phones—everything electronic that requires some sort of code for access. Websites, automated shipping products, e-mails, all of those apps—and even some of the vehicles out there now—all require some sort of password.

These properties are as important as our homes these days.

Many apps can help us with our passwords. If you like them, use them, but make sure that the password is noted for that app. See what I mean? LOL!

You can also do a bit of housekeeping for these types of membership accounts. If you don't use them, delete them. It will be so much easier for you and the person taking care of things for you. For example, if you don't use all of your streaming accounts, delete the ones you don't use. Same goes for all those shopping websites you had to subscribe to so that they would let you into their website. If you haven't shopped there for a while, delete it. If you want to shop there again, you can set up another membership when and if you need something from them later on. This will streamline things.

PROPERTY INFORMATION KEY

Home Address: _____

City: _____ Postal Code: _____

Own: ___ Property Roll #: _____

Rent: ___ Landlord's Contact Info: _____

Mailbox Location (Street Name): _____ Box #: _____

Property/Contents Insurance Co: _____

Policy #: _____ Contact Tel #: _____

Hydro/Electric Account: _____

Natural Gas/Propane Account: _____

Water Account: _____

Cellular Account: _____

Telephone Account: _____

2nd Home: ___ Location: _____

Province/State: _____ Postal/Zip Code: _____

Management Company: _____

Vehicle: _____ VIN #: _____

Insurance Company: _____

Contact Tel #: _____ Policy #: _____

Vehicle: _____ VIN #: _____

Insurance Company: _____

Contact Tel #: _____ Policy #: _____

(If you need more space for details, please use the back pages)

Password Protected Property

Website   Username   Password

_____

_____

_____

_____

_____

_____

_____

_____

_____

_____

_____

_____

_____

_____

(If you need more space for details, please use the back pages)

Chapter 7

Professional Information Key

Power of attorney: A power of attorney (POA) is a legal document that gives one party the legal authority to act on another's behalf to manage legal and financial affairs. The power can be very broad to allow complete control over all finances and property, or it can be limited to a specific task. As there are many types of POA, please seek legal advice on what's best for your family situation.

Will: A will or testament is a legal document that expresses a person's wishes as to how their property will be distributed after the death and which person will manage the property until its final distribution.

Please understand the laws where you live. Each state, province and country have its own laws relating to a power of attorney and a will.

As I mentioned in *The Family Connection Guide*, we just don't like to talk about this subject! Our parents' generations just didn't. Period! They felt that it was nobody's business, and it didn't matter who knew what. Everyone would find out when they had left this world. They never thought about anyone taking care of things but them.

The world has definitely changed, and we need to change our mindset about it.

I have spoken to many people about this subject, and what I heard is that they don't understand the legal terms and get frustrated and walk away. I get it. Some of the legal mumbo-jumbo is nuts and can make your head spin. It has to be explained in simple English terms.

I think this profession knows that the legal wording scares most people from getting things in place and having a simple plan. That was one of the main reasons I created *The Family Connection Guide* and this book, *The Keeper of The Gate*.

There are just too many what-ifs when you don't have a will in place. Do yourself a favour; speak to a lawyer and get the information that fits your family's situation. Most or some lawyers, will give you a free 30-minute in-person, on-the-phone or Zoom call. Meeting with a lawyer can give you some of the information you are not sure of. You'll feel so much better making progress.

I have met with a few lawyers while I was writing *The Family Connection Guide,* and all of them are more than willing to meet with you and give you the basics of writing a will and appointing a POA for health and financial matters depending on your family situation.

In the many conversations I have had with friends, many had an idea of what would happen if they were no longer here in this world, and many were wrong in their thinking, including me.

Every family is different, and many families have dynamics that can pan out in many ways. Search "what happens if I die without a will." You won't believe some of the stories. This is the reason to speak to a lawyer. At least get the correct information of what can happen if there is nothing in place. It can get nasty, ridiculous and petty. It can go on for what feels like forever if things are not in place.

From everyone who has gone through a family dynamic situation, I am sure they will tell you to get something in place.

PROFESSIONAL INFORMATION KEY

I mentioned in my Introduction that this book is for a short-term absence from being the Keeper of your Gate—a day or two, maybe a week or so. But if it would be a longer or indefinite period of time, you need to have something in place. What I am speaking of is a POA, power of attorney. There are many different types of POAs and what they can do. For instance, there are Financial POAs and Healthcare POAs. As the definition says, it can be very broad or very limited to a specific task.

If you are responsible for anyone in your family who has a disability or special needs, and you are no longer able to manage their day-to-day, you will need to have something in place for that person. I can't stress this enough. Look it up online. Many different scenarios can happen, depending on the laws where you live.

At least have a conversation with a lawyer to have the basics, and get started with a plan. Even if you don't have it all figured out and only have a basic idea of what you need, it's better than not having anything at all. You can always make adjustments to your plan as things change over time. Government programs are changing all the time, and your goals will need to change with them.

I have had many discussions with people who have bought my first book, *The Family Connection Guide*, and are asking me if I know the lawyers who will give them 30 minutes or more of their time for advice on what type of POA and wills they should have in place. I am working on a few things to have a list available for anyone who buys my books through my website. It's a large list, so stay tuned for that information.

PROFESSIONAL INFORMATION KEY

Lawyer: _____

Contact Info: _____

E-mail: _____

Last Visit: _____

Accountant: _____

Contact Info: _____

E-mail: _____

Last Visit: _____

Documentation

Power of Attorney Medical: Yes ____ No ____

Name: _____ Contact #: _____

Power of Attorney Financial: Yes ____ No ____

Name: _____ Contact #: _____

Last Will & Testament: Yes___ No____   Birth Certificate: Yes____ No____

Location of Documentation: _____

Other Professional Contacts: _____

_____

_____

_____

If you require more space, please use the back pages, Additional Details.

Afterword

"The number one benefit of being organized is less stress."

Lifewithlessmess.com

We know there are many reasons for disorganization, including the way we process our daily tasks, our belief systems, thinking that we lack skill sets and, the biggest one, perfectionism!

I am definitely a perfectionist, or I was. I used to have the cleanest, most organized desk, but an associate told me that a clean desk is great, but if you spend too much time on it, you won't have the time to put anything on it. Meaning, I was too worried about the look of my desk and not worried enough about my job.

That sat with me for a long time. I am still pretty organized. I have a friend who always jokes with me about my linen closet and how my towels are folded to perfection. She would always say "No one is going to look in your closet!" To this day, we still laugh about it. She sends me funny videos of cats folding fitted sheets.

I guess what I'm trying to say is that being organized doesn't mean being perfect. It means, to me, anyway, that I have all my t's crossed and my i's dotted. I don't like to waste time trying to figure something out when I have the time to be prepared for it in the first place. I get angry with myself for procrastinating, saying to myself that there's time for this, that or the other thing. Then the time comes that I need to get it done, and now I'm rushing to complete whatever the task is. Not everyone is like that, and life gets in the way. It's not something to stress about, but why not have things in place if you have the tools to be ready for an unfortunate event?

We all have roles to play in our relationships. Being prepared for any event—be it a party, work, family milestone or an *unexpected* emergency—we have a responsibility to be the best we can be. Did that sound silly or what?

I believe everyone cares about being prepared, but they have not gotten around to it or don't know where to start. Recently, I have found that an increasing number of people have no idea what they need to know until they are under pressure and in a crisis situation, losing precious time while scrambling to find the important documents to temporarily keep things in their lives in order. Small mistakes lead to many mistakes if you don't take the time to be organized. Don't hit that wall! If this is the case for you, make the time and complete these forms, and be better prepared for your next family crisis.

I made the time, and so should you. Let's do this!

"For every minute spent organizing, an hour is earned"

Benjamin Franklin

All the very best to you and your family,

Beth

AFTERWORD

I'd love to hear from you or if you have any questions, please email me at

beth@thefamilyconnectionguide.com

www.thefamilyconnectionguide.com

Additional Details

Use this page for other important information or if you need additional space.

Additional Details

Use this page for other important information or if you need additional space.

Additional Details

Use this page for other important information or if you need additional space.

Additional Details

Use this page for other important information or if you need additional space.

Additional Details

Use this page for other important information or if you need additional space.

Additional Details

Use this page for other important information or if you need additional space.

www.ingramcontent.com/pod-product-compliance
Lightning Source LLC
Chambersburg PA
CBHW051332110526
44590CB00032B/4490